Persuading
People

Pocket Mentor Series

The *Pocket Mentor* Series offers immediate solutions to common challenges managers face on the job every day. Each book in the series is packed with handy tools, self-tests, and real-life examples to help you identify your strengths and weaknesses and hone critical skills. Whether you're at your desk, in a meeting, or on the road, these portable guides enable you to tackle the daily demands of your work with greater speed, savvy, and effectiveness.

Books in the series:

Leading Teams
Running Meetings
Managing Time
Managing Projects
Coaching People
Giving Feedback
Leading People
Negotiating Outcomes
Writing for Business
Giving Presentations
Understanding Finance
Dismissing an Employee
Creating a Business Plan
Managing Stress
Delegating Work
Shaping Your Career
Persuading People

Persuading People

Expert Solutions to Everyday Challenges

Harvard Business Press

Boston, Massachusetts

No part of this publication may be reproduced, stored in or introduced into a re-trieval system, or transmitted, in any form, or by any means (electronic, mechanical, photocopying, recording, or otherwise), without the prior permission of the pub-lisher. Requests for permission should be directed to permissions@hbsp.harvard.edu, or mailed to Permissions, Harvard Business School Publishing, 60 Harvard Way, Boston, Massachusetts 02163.

Library of Congress Cataloging-in-Publication Data
Persuading people : expert solutions to everyday challenges.
    p. cm. — (Pocket mentor series)
    Includes bibliographical references.
    ISBN-13: 978-1-4221-2273-0
    1. Persuasion (Psychology)—Social aspects. 2. Persuasion (Rhetoric)
    HM1196.P466 2008
    303.3'42—dc22
                                                    2007042334

The paper used in this publication meets the requirements of the American National Standard for Permanence of Paper for Publications and Documents in Libraries and Archives Z39.48-1992.

Contents

Tips and Tools   65

Mentor's Message: Why Master the Art and Science of Persuasion?

You know them—those talented persuaders who somehow manage to convince everyone around them to support their great ideas. Persuasive people generate real value for their companies by turning ideas into action.

Yet many managers view persuasion as manipulation. Properly used, persuasion isn't manipulation at all. Instead, it can be the process of changing or reinforcing others' attitudes and behaviors to serve important business needs.

Think about it: in a single day on the job, you might lobby for funding for your department, pitch a new product's benefits to a customer, and convince a supplier to expedite an order. In each of these situations, you need persuasion to get the results you want.

Persuasion is a blend of art and science. To achieve this blend, you need to master a range of skills, including building your credibility, winning others' minds and hearts, and overcoming resistance to your ideas. If you sharpen these skills, you'll sweeten the odds of transforming your own excellent ideas into valuable business outcomes. This guide shows you how.

Harry Mills, Mentor

Harry Mills is author of twenty-six books on sales, negotiation, and influence, including the best-selling titles *Artful Persuasion: How to Command Attention, Change Minds, and Influence People*; *The Street-Smart Negotiator*; and *Power Points!* He advises companies how to use the tools and techniques of persuasion to close complex deals and develop leadership skills.

Harry is also chief executive of The Mills Group, an international consulting and training company, whose clients include IBM, PricewaterhouseCoopers, KPMG, Ernst & Young, Unilever, Toyota, and Oracle. He can be contacted at harry.mills@millsonline.com. The Mills Group's Web sites are www.millsonline.com and www.drillingfordiamonds.com.

Persuading People: The Basics

Understanding Persuasion

TALENTED PERSUADERS HAVE the power to capture an audience, sway others' opinions, and convert opponents to their cause. They wield influence and eloquence to convince others to align with their perspectives, support their positions or ideas, and help implement their solutions. But what exactly is persuasion, and why is it important in the business world? Let's find out.

What is persuasion?

Persuasion is a process that enables you to change or reinforce others' attitudes, opinions, or behaviors. It can take place in a single meeting or over time through a series of discussions. Persuasion is a skill that's essential for success in all relationships—personal and business alike. What's more, persuasion is a matter not only of making a rational case but also of presenting information in a way that appeals to fundamental human emotions. It's about positioning an idea, approach, or solution in a way that appeals to the people who are affected by it.

In many ways, persuasion blends art and science. It's an art in that it requires the ability to establish trust and strong communication skills. It's a science in that it hinges on the disciplined collection and analysis of information and solidly researched principles of human behavior. By leveraging proven techniques, anyone can enhance his or her persuasion skills.

Why is persuasion important?

The applications of persuasion are virtually infinite. An employee lobbying for a pay raise, a sales manager pitching the benefits of a new product line to a customer, a purchasing manager convincing a supplier to expedite shipment of an order—these are only a few examples of persuasion situations. Many people, without even realizing it, draw on their persuasion skills every day.

Profound changes in the business world have made persuasion a more critical managerial skill than ever. Here are examples:

- The days of a command-and-control leadership style have given way to a business world increasingly characterized by cross-functional teams of peers, joint ventures, and inter-company partnerships.

- In some countries, many young people now entering the workforce have come to maturity questioning authority.

- With the advent of electronic communication and globalization, ideas and people are flowing more freely than ever within and across organizations.

Clearly, formal authority no longer gets managers as far as it used to. To do their jobs—accomplishing work through others—managers must persuade others rather than simply issue orders.

"The best way to shape the future is to influence it."
—Harry Mills

What Would YOU Do?

Persuade Me, Baby

A FEW MONTHS AGO, Margaret was promoted to manager of facilities and land use. Recently, she read an interesting article about a new on-site child care program that many other companies like hers are implementing. Margaret believes that this program would save the company money and generate more choices for employees, and she'd like to convince her supervisor and other key players in the company of the program's value. She feels certain that her organization would be better off implementing the new program.

But the company has a culture of maintaining a distinct separation between employees' personal and professional lives, and Margaret suspects that she may encounter some resistance to her idea.

What would YOU do? The mentor will suggest a solution in *What You COULD Do*.

Key elements of persuasion

Persuasion is a complex process that requires careful preparation, back-and-forth dialogue, and a deep understanding of how people make decisions. Skilled persuaders engage in a mutual process of learning and negotiating with their audience. They focus on these four critical areas:

- **Credibility.** Skilled persuaders establish their own credibility by acquiring expertise as well as building and cultivating positive, trusting relationships.

- **Common ground.** Effective persuaders frame goals on common ground, describing the benefits of the position they're advocating in terms of what they value and what others value.

- **Supporting information.** Persuasive managers reinforce their positions with striking data mixed with compelling stories, examples, and images.

- **Deep understanding of emotion.** Talented persuaders understand and connect with the feelings of their audience.

Ethical considerations

Persuasion is most effective when it's based on mutual gain and ethical behaviors. Ethical persuaders recognize the opportunities for mutual gain inherent in any situation. They legitimately leverage these opportunities to create win–win solutions. They also consider the long-term implications of everything they do. They know that unethical tactics can instantly destroy a reputation of trust and credibility built over years.

Unfortunately, some persuaders use unethical behaviors. They exploit opportunities to deceive and manipulate others. For them, persuasion is a contest in which they win—and you lose. Such individuals focus on closing the short-term deal. They don't care how their behavior today might damage their reputation tomorrow. And they fail to build proposals based on mutual gain. In the long term, of course, these are losing strategies.

"To be persuasive, we must be believable. To be believable, we must be credible. To be credible, we must be truthful."
—Edward R. Murrow

What You COULD Do.

Remember Margaret's dilemma about proposing a new on-site child care program at her company?

Here's what the mentor suggests:

Before presenting her idea, Margaret needs to establish her credibility in the minds of her supervisors and peers. She also needs to decide who has the power to approve or reject her idea, who would be most affected by a change to the new program, and who most influences these decision makers and stakeholders.

Once she has identified these various audience members, Margaret should assess their receptivity to her idea and their willingness to take the actions required to approve and implement it. Based on her assessment, she then needs to structure her presentation in ways that appeal to her listeners and emphasize the advantages they value. She also needs to anticipate and determine how she will address possible resistance.

Building Your Credibility

CREDIBILITY IS THE cornerstone of persuasion. Without it, your audience won't commit time or resources to considering your idea or proposal. Your credibility manifests itself on two levels:

- **Your ideas.** Are your ideas sound? For example, does your notion for a new product make sense in light of current market conditions and business concerns? Have you thought through all the ramifications?

- **You as a person.** Are you believable? Trustworthy? Sincere? Have you proven yourself knowledgeable and well informed? For instance, if you've proposed a new product, do you have a solid understanding of its specifications, target markets, customers, and competition? Can others perceive that understanding?

Credibility can be expressed as this simple, powerful formula:

$$Credibility = Trust + Expertise$$

The more trust you earn and expertise you accumulate, the more credible you *and* your ideas become.

Winning others' trust

When you fail to earn trust, listeners discount most—if not all—of what you say. By contrast, when people trust you and your ideas, they tend to see you as believable, well informed, and sincere. They know that you have their best interests at heart. They also view you as possessing a strong emotional character (steady temperament) and integrity (honesty and reliability). Those qualities reinforce your appeal, and that in turn makes people more inclined to accept your ideas.

How do you earn others' trust? Here are several ways:

- **Be sincere.** Demonstrate your conviction that your idea is worth others' time and attention. When people see you as sincere and committed, they will more likely trust you.

- **Build a track record of trustworthiness.** Follow through on the promises and commitments you've made. Share or give credit to those who contribute good ideas. Present consistent values. By *behaving* in a trustworthy manner, you earn a reputation for *being* trustworthy.

- **Encourage the exploration of ideas.** To encourage dialogue and demonstrate your openness to others' perspectives, listen to their concerns. Establish an environment where all your colleagues can share their ideas and know that their opinions are valued.

- **Put others' best interests first.** When people believe that you have their interests in mind, they tend to trust you and your ideas. For instance, suppose a marketing director helps a valued subordinate get promoted to a different department. Although the marketing director knows it's difficult to lose a top-notch team member, she accepts that her job includes helping others develop their professional skills. In addition to helping her subordinate, the marketing director earns the trust of her subordinate *and* the other department head—trust that may come in handy in the future.

- **Use candor.** When you own up to your flaws, people see you as a truthful person—on the assumption that most individuals try to conceal their faults. Thus, an honest acknowledgment of any weaknesses in your proposal can help build trust with your audience.

Demonstrating your expertise

Like trust, expertise enables you to build credibility. People see you as having expertise when you exercise sound judgment that proves you're knowledgeable about your ideas. You also demonstrate expertise by accumulating a history of successes.

To build or strengthen your expertise, consider the following guidelines:

- **Research your ideas.** Find out everything you can about the idea you are proposing—by talking with knowledgeable individuals, reading relevant sources, and so on. Collect pertinent data and information to support and contradict your idea so that you are well versed on your idea's strengths and weaknesses.

- **Get firsthand experience.** Ask to be assigned to a team that will provide new insights into particular markets or products.

- **Cite trusted sources.** Back your position with knowledge gained from respected business or trade periodicals, books, independently produced reports, lectures, and experts within or outside your organization.

- **Prove it.** Launch small pilot projects to demonstrate that your ideas deserve serious consideration. For example, if you're advocating a new customer-service process for your department, conduct a limited experiment with the process to generate firsthand information about its benefits.

- **Master the terminology.** Demonstrate that you know the verbal shorthand used by the people in your audience. During meetings, industry conferences, and other business gatherings, listen closely for buzzwords. Make sure you understand their meaning—and use them appropriately in your business communications.

- **Don't hide your credentials.** If appropriate, let people know about any advanced degrees you've earned. For example, a personal trainer who is launching a line of nutritional supplements would want to advertise her degree in nutrition along with her credentials as a licensed physical therapist. Note, though, that in some organizations, publicizing academic credentials is considered bad form. Doing so might hurt your credibility if your colleagues firmly believe that it's a person's ideas that count, and not her degrees. If this describes your company's culture, think of all your relevant experience and knowledge that inform and support your idea.

Then relate that experience and knowledge at appropriate opportunities to those with any influence or stake in your proposal.

- **Hire independent authorities.** Retain the services of an industry consultant or recognized outside expert to advocate your position. The authority's credibility will augment your own.

- **Gather endorsements.** Publicize accolades you've won for work related to your proposal, such as e-mails or letters of praise from satisfied customers, superiors, and peers. Be diplomatic in your self-promotion to avoid appearing arrogant or boastful and thus undermining support.

By establishing your trustworthiness *and* expertise, you build the credibility you need to get your audience's attention and interest.

Understanding
Your Audience

I N SOME PERSUASION situations, you present your proposal to one person; in others, to several or many individuals at a time. In either case, your true audience usually consists of several kinds of people: decision makers (people who approve or reject your idea), key stakeholders (those directly affected by the acceptance of your proposal), and influencers (those who can influence or persuade the stakeholders and decision makers).

Distinguishing three types of audience members

Most persuasion situations involve several **decision makers**. For example, if you want to hire an additional employee for your unit and you're lobbying your supervisor for the funds, he may not be the only decision maker you need to persuade. His boss may have the final say on new hires.

To identify key **stakeholders,** think of all the individuals who stand to be affected by acceptance of your proposal. In most cases, key stakeholders include not only the person to whom you're presenting your proposal but also individuals such as peers, subordinates, customers, superiors, and board members.

Influencers often participate in the decision-making process by providing advice and information to key stakeholders and decision makers. For example, if you're trying to persuade a marketing manager to launch a new Web campaign, she might invite the head of information technology to participate in a meeting so that she can ask him questions and get his opinion on the matter. The head of IT in this case is an influencer.

Once you've identified all the individuals who make up your true audience, it's time to analyze their receptivity.

Analyzing listeners' receptivity

Audiences differ in what they know about your proposal or idea, how interested they are in what you have to say, and how strongly they support your views—all of which influence their receptivity. To analyze audience receptivity, take these actions:

- **Monitor reactions.** Look for signs of openness or resistance to you or your ideas in e-mails and other formal or informal communication from your intended listeners.

- **Assess body language.** Notice your listeners' tone of voice and body language during casual hallway conversations and other brief, informal exchanges. Does your intended audience seem interested in your ideas? Distracted by other concerns? Skeptical?

- **Talk with others.** Identify key influencers and other individuals who have a finger on the pulse of your audience's moods and expectations regarding important upcoming developments in the company. Ask these individuals for their thoughts about your listeners' likely receptivity to your idea. Ask them what they and the key decision makers and stakeholders value and care about most, as well as what benefits they see in your idea.

RECEPTIVITY *n* **1:** an audience's openness to a persuader and his or her ideas.

Audiences generally fall within one of six categories of receptivity. The table "Audience receptivity and persuasion strategies" shows these categories, along with their corresponding persuasion strategies.

Audience receptivity and persuasion strategies

Audience type	Persuasion strategies
Hostile—disagrees with you	• Use humor or a story to warm them up to you. • Focus on areas you agree on. • Demonstrate your expertise, and cite experts. • Support statements with solid evidence. • Stress that you're looking for a win–win outcome. • Identify benefits they would value.
Neutral—understands your position but still needs convincing	• Spell out your proposition's benefits to listeners. • Present just three clear, compelling points, backed by expert evidence, data, and concrete examples.

Audience type	Persuasion strategies
Neutral—understands your position but still needs convincing (*cont.*)	• Use stories, personal experiences, and anecdotes to appeal to their emotions. • Point out any downside of not accepting your proposal. • Discuss the alternatives you've considered or you believe others might raise.
Uninterested—informed about your subject but doesn't care about it	• Grab their attention with a heart-stopping story, headline, or fact. • Show how the topic affects them. • Support your case with three to five compelling facts backed by expert testimony or statistics.
Uninformed—lacks information needed to become convinced	• Establish your credibility by showcasing your experience or qualifications. • Keep your presentation simple and straightforward; don't confuse them with complex evaluations. • Create an emotional link by sharing several personal anecdotes.
Supportive—already agrees with you	• Recharge their enthusiasm with success stories and vivid testimonials. • Help them anticipate and refute possible arguments from opponents. • Hand out a detailed action plan with clear deadlines.
Mixed—contains a cross section of attitudes and views	• Identify listeners whom you most have to win over and who have the most power. Concentrate your efforts on them. • Appeal to different subgroups with different messages; for example, snack-food commercials promise kids great taste and promise parents good nutrition. • Avoid promising everything to everyone.

Understanding audience members' decision-making styles

To further boost your odds of persuading those who have the power to accept or reject your proposal, tailor your arguments to fit their decision-making style. People have distinct styles of decision making. The table "Decision-making styles and persuasion strategies" lists five styles, their characteristics, and corresponding persuasion strategies.

How do you know which style your decision makers possess? As you did when analyzing your audience's receptivity, observe decision makers' behavior in meetings and hallway conversations and examine their communication for hints.

If your audience includes decision makers with whom you have little or no direct contact, learn about their decision-making habits through whatever means are available, such as others in the organization, news sources, public meetings, and so on.

Decision-making styles and persuasion strategies

Decision-making style	Decision maker's characteristics	Persuasion strategies
Charismatic	• Initially enthralled, but bases final decisions on balanced information • May mislead you into thinking you've scored an immediate success	• Focus discussion on results. • Make simple, straightforward arguments. • Use visual aids to demonstrate features and benefits of proposal.

Decision-making style	Decision maker's characteristics	Persuasion strategies
Thinker	• Cerebral, logical, and risk-averse • Needs extensive detail	• Gather as much supporting data as possible. • Use a fact-based approach to persuasion.
Skeptic	• Challenges every data point • Decides based on gut feelings	• Establish as much credibility as possible. • At the beginning of a meeting, invite them to challenge you—indicating that you value their ideas and will use them to create the final idea or proposal.
Follower	• Relies on own or others' past decisions to make choices • Takes plenty of time to decide whether to adopt idea • Follows the lead of bosses or others who are politically important	• Focus on proven methods such as references and testimonials. • Understand whom they like to follow or defer to, and get that person's support.
Controller	• Unemotional and analytical • Abhors uncertainty • Inclined to implement only her own ideas	• Ensure that your argument is sound and well structured. • Identify outcomes of value to them.

Steps for Reading Your Audience Quickly

1. **Scan the surrounding environment.**

   Browse the audience; look for general patterns in people's appearance and behavior. What is the overall mood of the gathering?

What's going on in the background that may be influencing your audience members?

For example, are there many distractions?

2. Identify key traits you want to read.

Focus on the person or individuals you want to read. Mentally draw up a list of several key traits you want to observe in those audience members.

For example, do you want to gain a sense of your listeners' energy levels, ability to focus on your message, and openness to new ideas? Do you want to gauge their emotional state and confidence levels?

3. Interpret behaviors.

Bring the key traits you identified in step 2 into sharper focus. Examine the behaviors associated with those traits in minute detail.

For example, to detect readiness to hear your message, observe whether your audience members are making eye contact with you, showing lively facial expressions, and nodding in agreement. To detect boredom or indifference, watch for blank stares, heads held in the palm of the hand, finger or foot tapping, and doodling. To detect openness, look for unfolded arms, warm smiles, leaning forward, and open palms.

4. Test your assumptions.

Look for ways to test your assumptions about the traits you observed in step 3.

For example, don't assume too quickly that leaning forward always signifies openness. For some individuals, that posture may mean they're having trouble hearing you. In this case, you might test your assumptions by asking, "Can everyone hear me okay?" And whereas drooping eyes or limited eye contact may indicate boredom in some people, those same behaviors may reveal fatigue in others—especially if you're presenting your case after lunch or first thing in the morning.

The key is to think about a *range* of possible meanings for the behaviors you're observing and test your conclusions to ensure that you're reading your audience as accurately as possible.

Winning Your Audience's Mind

REASON *AND* EMOTIONS play major roles in the way people make business decisions. To persuade others, you thus need to win your listeners' minds and their hearts. In this chapter, we focus on appealing to your audience members' minds. You can do this in several ways:

- The way you structure your presentation

- The evidence you provide to back up your proposal

- The benefits of your idea that you emphasize

- The words you use

Structuring your presentation effectively

How do you decide what to say first, second, and so on in making a persuasive proposal? Sometimes your assessment of your audience's receptivity will influence the structure you select. At other times, your subject matter will suggest the appropriate structure. And you might decide to use one structure to present your case to one audience (for example, a receptive group) and another to present the same case to another audience (such as a skeptical audience).

Consider the following examples of structures:

- **Problem and solution.** Describe a pressing problem, and then solve it by presenting a convincing solution. Use this structure with an uninterested audience or one that's uninformed about the problem.

- **Presentation of both sides and then refutation.** To win over neutral or hostile audiences, argue both sides. First present your opponents' side, thereby showing that you accept the validity of their position and increasing their receptivity. Then refute their case by challenging their evidence and disproving their arguments.

- **Cause and effect.** Discuss the causes underlying a problem, and then show how your idea will remove those causes. Or emphasize the undesirable effects of a problem, and then explain how your proposal will mitigate those effects. Use this structure for mixed audiences.

- **Motivational sequence.** Capture your audience's attention with a startling statistic, anecdote, or joke—and then identify a pressing need. Explain how your proposal will satisfy that need, and help listeners visualize the bright future in store if they adopt your proposal. Finally, tell your audience the actions you want them to take. Use this structure for supportive audiences.

How you begin and end your presentation is especially critical. Get your audience's attention right away with a dynamic opening. Conclude with a call for action in which you clearly indicate what you want from your listeners.

Providing compelling evidence

The evidence you provide to support your proposal—such as testimonials, examples, statistics, and graphical evidence—can strengthen your persuasiveness.

- **Testimonials** enhance persuasiveness when they come from sources your audience considers expert and credible. For instance, if you're advocating the adoption of a new technology, provide quotations from companies similar to yours that have adopted the technology with excellent results.

- **Examples** capture people's attention by turning generalizations and abstractions into concrete proof. To illustrate, cite examples of what a proposed new technology can accomplish.

- **Statistics** become especially effective if you make them understandable and memorable. How? Help people grasp the meaning of large numbers. For instance, to convey $1 trillion, say, "If you were to count a trillion one-dollar bills— one every second, 24 hours a day—it would take you thirty-two years." Personalize numbers: "Four out of ten people in this room exaggerate their expenses." Cite jaw-dropping comparisons: "Our main competitor processes orders fifty times faster than we do."

- **Graphical evidence,** such as slides, flip charts, videotapes, and product samples, can boost your success. That's because three-quarters of what people learn they acquire visually. Choose a medium that's appropriate to your message; convey one concept per slide or other visual; and consider the psychological impact of colors. (Red, for example, means "We're in debt" to financial managers, but to engineers is signifies that a wire has electricity running through it.) Also, when you create charts and tables, first determine the main trends or patterns you want to emphasize, and then take care not to distort or misrepresent information.

Tip: Make your statistics credible by citing reputable, authoritative, unbiased sources. Also, round off numbers. Most people find it much easier to visualize and remember "three million" than "3,168,758," or "about 30 percent" than "31.69 percent."

When carefully selected and compellingly presented, evidence in all its forms can help your audience see how reasonable your idea really is.

"The real message isn't what you say. It's what the other person remembers."
   —Harry Mills

Answering your audience's question "What's in it for me?"

The **features** of your idea—such as how a new computer you're advocating works—may interest your listeners. But its **benefits**—how the idea will *help* your audience members and make their lives better—most strongly attract listeners' attention. Persuaders who fail to answer their listeners' question "What's in it for me?" stand little chance of winning their minds.

To understand this firsthand, consider the table "Features and benefits," which lists a computer's features and benefits. Which column do *you* find most appealing?

Each benefit may appeal to listeners on one of two primary levels of motivation: the desire for gain and the fear of loss.

- A benefit may enable listeners to gain something they don't currently have—for example, money, time, popularity, possessions, or a good reputation.

- A benefit may enable listeners to avoid losing something they currently have.

Research shows that the fear of loss is actually a more powerful motivator than the prospect of gain. For example, the fear of losing money you already have is a more powerful motivator than the thought of gaining money you don't have!

Think about which benefits your audience would value most. Then develop a **unique value proposition** for your proposal by asking these questions:

- What benefits does my proposal provide? What will my audience members gain? What will they avoid losing?

- What evidence shows that these benefits are real? Are there compelling and credible testimonials, examples, statistics, and graphical representations available?

- What makes my proposal unique? What's different and unusual about my idea? Why should my audience accept my proposal and not others'?

By spotlighting the unique advantages of your proposition, you convince listeners that your idea merits their serious consideration.

UNIQUE VALUE PROPOSITION *n* **1:** the essence of your idea; what makes your idea unique and better than alternative or competing proposals, and how it will benefit your intended audience.

Features and benefits

Features	Benefits
The latest microprocessor	Lets you work faster and use the latest applications
A 10-gigabyte hard drive	Enables you to store more data and access and update it faster
A flat-screen monitor	Makes it easier to view more, while occupying less desk space than traditional monitors

1. **Brainstorm your proposition's benefits.**

   Think about all the possible benefits of your proposition. Ask your-self what your audience would gain and what it would avoid losing by accepting your proposition. Research suggests that the fear of loss is a more powerful motivator than the prospect of gain.

2. **Prioritize the benefits based on your audience's interests.**

   Review your responses to step 1. Of the benefits you've identified, which do you think your audience values most? Prioritize audience members' interests based on what you know about them—your understanding of their current problems, concerns, and values.

3. **Gather evidence showing that the high-priority benefits are real.**

   Collect compelling testimonials from credible sources showing that the benefits that matter most to your audience members are within their reach if they accept your proposition. In addition, gather examples, statistics, and graphical representations that speak to the benefits of your proposition.

   For instance, suppose you want to persuade your sales team to use a new process for contacting customers. You might cite successful results that seasoned sales teams have obtained by using the new process, and you might show an example of how one salesperson used the process to acquire new customers. You could also use a chart or other graphic to depict the rise in sales that other compa-nies have achieved by using the process.

4. **Decide what makes your proposal unique.**

   Compare your idea against potential alternative propositions. Ask yourself what's different, unusual, and superior about your idea. Why should your audience accept your proposal and not others'?

   Be ready to explain in succinct, compelling terms what makes your proposal better than others.

Choosing the right words

The words you select can strongly determine whether your listeners consider your proposal. For example, see the table "The right words."

Whenever possible—and only when appropriate to your audience—sprinkle attention-grabbing words, such as *easy, free, guaranteed, proven,* and *results,* throughout your persuasion communication. Most of these are borrowed from sales, and, despite their heavy use, they're an effective, tried-and-true tactic.

Tip: Vary your speaking pace to suit your purpose. Speaking fast helps you excite and energize your audience, whereas a slow pace creates a mood of anticipation. For most of your presentation, the best pace is slow enough for listeners to follow but quick enough to sustain their interest.

The right words

Your selection of words	Example of what to say	Example of what *not* to say
Affirmative language, communicating precisely what you expect to happen	"*When* you finish that report, we'll celebrate by going out for a pizza."	"If you finish that report, we'll celebrate by going out for a pizza."
Assertive speech, presenting your arguments with confidence	"*I believe* that our project needs additional funding."	"*I would guess* that our project needs additional funding."
Win–win language that fosters cooperation	"That's a new approach. *Let's talk it through* to see where we end up."	"Maybe you should *run* some numbers, *because I don't see that working.*"
Phrasing that makes people trust your integrity	"*This is a much better deal* for you than the previous one."	"*To be perfectly honest*, I think this deal is perfect for you."

Tip: Use concrete language that is clear and to the point. As much as possible, avoid abstract, ambiguous, and wordy language. For example, it is more effective to say, "Sales dropped 10 percent this year" than to say, "At certain points in the year, sales numbers were up, then they were down, causing an overall negative impact on forecasted numbers."

Capturing Your Audience's Heart

THE MOST LOGICAL argument won't persuade people unless you've also connected with them on an emotional level. In fact, emotions play an even more powerful role in human decision making than facts, numbers, and a rational assessment of a proposal's benefits. Why? Here are several reasons:

- Emotionally evocative presentations—such as gripping stories—are more interesting and memorable than statistics and facts.

- Emotion tends to prompt behavioral changes more quickly than logical appeals do. Responding emotionally requires less effort on the part of listeners than logically weighing the pros and cons of a presentation.

- Emotionally arousing arguments distract people from noticing the speaker's intention to persuade.

In the most successful persuasive situations, people *first* accept the presenter's proposal unconsciously, based on their emotional response. *Then* they justify their decision based on a logical assessment of the facts.

Four tools can help you appeal to your listeners' feelings: vivid descriptions, metaphors, analogies, and stories.

Using vivid descriptions

Vivid descriptions—words that paint evocative images in people's minds—deeply tap in to listeners' emotions. For example, suppose you want to persuade your supervisor to approve a new policy that will enable some employees to telecommute several days each week. You anticipate that your supervisor will worry that telecommuting may reduce worker productivity.

To persuade him otherwise, you vividly describe team members working diligently from their home offices, free of the many distractions that crop up in the office on a typical workday. You contrast that picture with one of employees being frequently interrupted by well-meaning coworkers who stop by to chat. As you paint these images in your supervisor's mind, he begins experiencing two emotions: a desire for a more focused, industrious staff, and an aversion to the disruptive reality you've described. He agrees to consider telecommuting as a viable alternative.

Leveraging the power of metaphor

A **metaphor** is an imaginative way of describing something as something else—for example, "Time is money." **Organizing metaphors** are overarching worldviews that shape a person's everyday actions—for instance, "Business is war."

People reveal their organizing metaphors through the language they use when speaking about the issue at hand. For example, a manager who sees business as war might say things like, "We can't

What Would YOU Do?

Drive That Point Home

B EN MANAGES A department of twenty people. He wants to persuade Molly, his supervisor, to approve a policy that will enable some employees to telecommute a day or two a week. Over the years, Ben has earned Molly's trust by consistently delivering on his workplace commitments and by attending to the organization's priorities. He has also acquired expertise in the area of telecommuting. In his previous job, he managed a group of employees who delivered excellent performance while occasionally working from home. He thus has clearly established credibility with Molly.

But he knows that to persuade her to approve the telecommuting policy, he'll also need to win her mind and heart. That is, he needs to both appeal to her powers of reason and tap in to her emotions. The trouble is, he's not sure where to begin.

What would YOU do? The mentor will suggest a solution in *What You COULD Do.*

concede ground," "We're being outflanked," or "We have to defend market share."

To change someone's organizing metaphor, follow these steps:

1. Identify a compelling replacement metaphor—for example, "Business is partnership." This metaphor focuses a business's efforts on building win-win relationships with key stakeholders rather than on defeating competitors.
2. Highlight the weaknesses of your audience's worldview using their metaphor. For example, "By focusing on competitors instead of customer support, we've allowed our customer-satisfaction levels to fall."
3. Provide examples of other companies that have achieved success using your replacement metaphor, as in "Company X's sales have increased 18 percent since the company appointed account managers to collaborate with the sales team."

Replacing someone's organizing metaphor is never easy; people cling tightly to their worldviews. But by providing powerful evidence of the flaws in an existing metaphor and the veracity of the new one, you can persuade others to at least consider a different outlook.

Making apt analogies

Analogies—comparisons between certain characteristics of things that otherwise are unalike—enable you to relate a new idea to one that's already familiar to your audience. Analogies engender feelings of familiarity, which many people find reassuring. Analogies also help people understand and therefore accept a new idea.

Steps for Introducing a New Organizing Metaphor

1. Observe your audience member.

Meet several times with the person you want to persuade, and talk about your idea or proposal. Jot down the common phrases and images he uses when speaking about the subject.

For example, suppose you're a customer-service manager and you need to persuade Frank, your subordinate, to use a new technology for processing orders. You suspect that Frank is resistant to the idea. You could mandate that Frank learn the new technology, but you know that he'll perform better with it if he truly embraces the idea.

You meet with Frank several times to discuss technology in general. During the conversations, Frank comments, "Those fancy gadgets have no soul," "You can't take the human touch out of business," and "Someday, none of us will have jobs anymore."

2. Translate the person's comments into a one-sentence metaphorical statement.

Ask yourself what the person's language highlights. What does it emphasize? What does it conceal? How would you capture the comments in a one-sentence metaphorical statement?

Returning to the example of Frank, you might translate his comments about technology into the following metaphor: "Technology is a heartless machine."

3. **Create a new metaphor to act as a frame for the changes you're proposing.**

    Think about various metaphors that might help the other person view the topic through a different lens.

    For instance, in Frank's case, you might come up with this new metaphor for technology: "Technology is a tool that frees people to provide even higher levels of customer service."

4. **Work to replace the person's current metaphor with your new one.**

    Think about how you might present your new metaphor to the person in a way that helps him adopt it. Your goal is to encourage the other person to make a "mindshift" without consciously realizing it. In short, you want to offer a new way of thinking that has clear advantages over the old way.

    How might you get Frank to view technology as a tool rather than a machine? Here are some ideas:

    - Share stories about how specific technologies have helped people become even more proficient at their jobs and master new skills that their companies value highly.
    - Present Frank with examples of how technologies have helped people solve customers' problems more easily and quickly— something that reinforces the "human touch" that Frank values.
    - Use specific language that helps Frank envision technology as a helpful tool that he can control to improve his own and others'

lives. For instance, "We're using technology *in the service* of our customers" and "We're *leveraging* technology to *sharpen* our skills and stay on the cutting edge of business."

Changing someone's mind-set isn't easy, so you will probably have to apply these kinds of techniques on multiple occasions to replace Frank's organizing metaphor with your new one.

Incongruous analogies and those that use humor are even more memorable. For example, when Benjamin Franklin once said, "Fish and visitors start to smell in three days," he delivered a vivid message of why people tire of visitors who outstay their welcome.

Sharing compelling stories

Stories also help make presentations come alive and drive messages home. They can accomplish the following:

- Grab listeners' attention with riveting plots and characters audiences can relate to

- Simplify complex ideas and make them concrete

- Evoke powerful emotions within listeners

- Stay in your audience's mind long after the facts have been forgotten

For instance, consider a product design manager who wants his team to generate innovative design ideas. His company is located in a region where many people have strong ties and allegiances to the local community. The manager evokes intense emotions in his team by telling the story of how outside competition is destroying businesses in his hometown. He tells of firms that have closed, childhood friends who have had to move, and office buildings that sit abandoned. He concludes his story by challenging his team to come up with ideas for "Made Here at Home" products. His team responds with a number of practical, innovative design ideas that tap local strengths and talents.

What You COULD Do.

Remember Ben's concern about how to win Molly's mind and heart?

Here's what the mentor suggests:

Ben could start winning Molly's mind by connecting telecommuting to business needs and results. For example, he could explain that telecommuting could decrease the department's high turnover. By letting people work from home occasionally, the department would gain their loyalty. He could also point to studies showing that companies that offer telecommuting, along with other work–life benefits, see productivity increases of 20 to 40 percent—and reductions in turnover of as much as 30 percent.

continued

To win Molly's heart, Ben could use stories or vivid examples to show how good things could be in their department if she supported telecommuting. Perhaps he could say something like, "Remember that time when you had to look after your mother—when she was ill and we were making arrangements for that conference? You could have easily done some of that work from home while taking care of your mom. But I remember you were worried about how it might look, since the company didn't have any clear policy on telecommuting. If we did have such a policy, you and others wouldn't have to worry anymore about how it looks. And, when necessary, we'd each be able to balance work and family obligations much more easily."

Overcoming Resistance from Listeners

Y OU'VE TAKEN STEPS to win your audience's minds and hearts—and yet you're still encountering resistance from some listeners. What's going on? The fact is that even the most carefully thought out and emotionally appealing proposal can meet with resistance. For any number of reasons, one or more of your listeners have made up their minds, and you simply can't sway them.

Resistance can stem from several sources. One listener may have committed to a strong position that diametrically opposes yours. Another may disagree with your idea on technical grounds. Yet another may resist for philosophical reasons; for example, he believes that commercial development should be minimized in favor of preserving park lands.

Resistance also takes many different forms—from head shaking to silent disagreement to outright verbal attacks—none of which translates into action supporting your plan.

How do you move resisters to your point of view? The key lies in understanding their positions and then presenting the benefits of your idea to them in terms of what they value.

The following guidelines can help:

- Identify resisters' interests.

- Understand resisters' emotions.

- Listen to resisters' concerns.

- Ensure consistent verbal and nonverbal messages.

- Present resisters' viewpoints before your own.

Identifying resisters' interests

Each person's unique life experiences shape her views of the world and influence how she responds to others' ideas. If you encounter resistance after presenting a proposal, avoid the temptation to keep pressing your case. Instead, think about what may be driving the person to disagree with you. Then adapt your response accordingly.

For example, suppose you want funding to conduct a study on the merits of entering a new market. The head of research and development (R&D) opposes your plan. She is concerned that entering a new market might direct company resources away from a project she wants to pursue. In this case, you might want to address her fears in your presentation, providing information on how entering a promising new market may generate more revenues for the company, which could in turn fund a broader range of new projects for the R&D group.

Tip: Draw conclusions for your listeners. Don't make your audience members guess your message. Help them arrive at the conclusions you want them to arrive at.

Understanding resisters' emotions and listening to their concerns

Most resistance springs from two emotions:

- **Fear.** Your audience doesn't like your idea because of its potential consequences. For instance, listeners may worry that a proposed restructuring will cost them their jobs.

- **Distrust.** Your audience doesn't like you or what you represent. For example, perhaps that R&D manager tends to view marketers as "artsy" and shortsighted.

By understanding the emotions driving resistance, you can take the next steps in addressing listeners' fears (for example, how likely is it that the restructuring will end in lost jobs?) or addressing their objections to you as a person so as to improve the relationship.

One powerful way to improve relationships is to build trust by listening closely to resisters' concerns. By listening, you demonstrate that you understand and value these individuals as well as their concerns and ideas. When people feel that they've been heard and that their ideas are valued, they become more open to considering your ideas.

The following techniques can help:

- **Paraphrase.** Mirror the resister's points. For example, "So you're saying that you think I'm just advancing the party line. Is that right?" Paraphrasing prompts your listener to respond with comments such as, "Well, yeah—I do." By getting the person to agree with you—even in this small way—you establish common ground, which can make the individual more receptive to your ideas.

- **Clarify the issues.** Identify the resister's primary concerns. For instance, "So what I hear you saying is that you have two main problems with my proposal. The first one you mentioned is probably the most important, right?" Again, you've established a level of understanding and agreement. You've also shown that you're capable of sorting out the vital issues.

"The Golden Rule of Persuasion—listen to others as you would have them listen to you."

—Harry Mills

Aligning your verbal and nonverbal messages

Check that your body language, tone of voice, and other aspects of nonverbal communication reinforce the spoken part of your message. If they don't, your resisters may view you as not credible or as conflicted about your position—two things that can stiffen their resistance.

For example, to telegraph confidence in your position, check that your posture is upright, your gestures assertive, your gaze direct, and your voice loud enough to be heard—but not so loud as to intimidate or annoy listeners.

Many successful persuaders rehearse nonverbal behaviors just as much as their spoken presentations. Effective persuaders also recognize when they are becoming overly emotional or angry—two behaviors that are inappropriate in many persuasion situations. They recover by openly acknowledging and apologizing for such behaviors. Having the courage to publicly admit a mistake in this way can help further establish trust and credibility.

Acknowledging resisters' viewpoints

If you suspect ahead of time that you'll encounter resistance from listeners, prepare a two-sided argument: theirs *and* yours. During your presentation, acknowledge your resisters' arguments *first*. You'll disarm these individuals by removing the opportunity for them to oppose you. Deprived of this opportunity, they'll be more open to discussion and may want to participate in solving the problem at hand.

Next, present *your* argument, clearly showing how it provides a more powerful solution than your opponents' argument does. When possible, show how you've incorporated resisters' ideas, interests, values, and concerns into your solution.

Understanding and using persuasion triggers

People respond to persuasion in two ways: consciously and unconsciously. If someone's in a *conscious mode*, he might respond thoughtfully to a proposal, weighing its pros and cons and attending carefully to the logic and content of the message.

In an ideal world, everyone would make decisions in this way. But in reality, many people don't have the time, information, or motivation to do so. Therefore, they switch their decision making to an *unconscious mode*, and this means that they spend less time processing information. They make decisions based more on instinct than on reason. And they resort to **persuasion triggers**, or mental shortcuts, to decide how to respond to a proposal.

"The advantage of emotions is that they lead us astray."
—Oscar Wilde

For example, Joe, a manager, might choose to accept a deal offered by Sue, a supplier's representative, instead of an idea offered by Bob—even though Sue's proposal is inferior to Bob's. Why? Joe likes Sue, and she once did him a favor.

You can further erode any resistance to your ideas by using persuasion triggers strategically. Researchers have identified seven persuasion triggers:

1. **Contrast.** Judgment is always relative. So when people make decisions, they often look for a benchmark to base their decisions on. For instance, suppose the first candidate you interview for a marketing manager position seems far too expensive when she asks for a starting salary of $89,000. Her request starts to look much more reasonable when you contrast her against the only other suitable candidate, who wants $110,000.

   To activate the contrast trigger, start by creating a benchmark to anchor the judgments of the person you need to persuade. Many salespeople do this by first showing you the most expensive item in a product line. This makes a midpriced item seem that much more affordable.

2. **Liking.** Human beings tend to accept the ideas of people they like. Liking, in turn, arises when people feel liked by another person and when they share something in common with him. For example, at direct sales engagements (where products are sold by a company representative in a person's home), invited guests (usually friends and neighbors of the host) buy more if they have a fondness for their host and feel that they share a bond with him.

How might you activate the liking trigger? Create bonds with peers, supervisors, and subordinates by informally discovering common interests—whether it's a shared alma mater, a passion for white-water rafting, or a love of cooking. Demonstrate your liking for others by expressing genuine compliments and making positive statements about their ideas, solutions, abilities, and qualities.

"Flattery will get you anywhere."
   —Jane Russell

3. **Reciprocity.** People feel a deep urge to repay favors in kind. This drive to reciprocate exists in all societies. For instance, when fund-raisers enclose a small, seemingly insignificant gift in an envelope to potential donors, the volume of donations increases markedly.

To activate the reciprocity trigger, the rule is to give before you ask. A small favor such as lending a fellow manager one of your staff members for a few days might be repaid fivefold when you later ask for that manager's support on an important project. In considering what to give, look for solutions that meet other individuals' interests and needs as well as your own.

4. **Social proof.** Individuals are more likely to follow another person's lead if what they are advocating is popular, standard practice, or part of a trend. A person who dresses or speaks much differently from her immediate colleagues or who comes from a markedly different culture usually starts with a persuasion handicap.

How do you activate the social proof trigger? Remember the power of association: make a connection (yourself, your company, or your product) to individuals and organizations your audience admires. Use peer power to influence horizontally, and not vertically. For instance, if you're trying to convince a group of resistant people of the merits of a new project, ask a respected company colleague who supports the initiative to speak up for it in a team meeting. You'll stand a better chance of persuading your colleagues with this person's testimony.

5. **Commitment and consistency.** People are more likely to embrace a proposal if they've made a voluntary, public, and written commitment to doing so. For example, 92 percent of residents of an apartment complex who signed a petition supporting a new recreation center later donated money to the cause.

To activate the commitment and consistency trigger, make others' commitments voluntary, public, and documented. Suppose, for instance, that you want to persuade an employee to submit reports on time. To inspire this behavior, make a link between the commitment and the person's values (mention its benefits for team spirit). Get that understanding in writing (a memo). And make the commitment public (mention your colleague's agreement with the memo).

6. **Authority.** Many people are trained from childhood to automatically obey the requests of authority figures such as parents, doctors, and police. Authority comes from a combination of a position and its associated credentials. For example, your authority as a manager in a drug company will be enhanced if you possess medical as well as business qualifications.

   Appropriate clothes or other trappings of authority can also increase the chances of successful persuasion. A businessperson who "power dresses" for an important presentation improves the odds that the pitch will be successful.

   To activate the authority trigger, make sure that the people you want to persuade are aware of the source of your authority. Also leverage appropriate clothing and other trappings of authority.

7. **Scarcity.** When something is in scarce supply—such as information, opportunities, and resources—people value it more. For instance, in one experiment, wholesale beef buyers were told that they were the only ones who had received information on a possible beef shortage. Their orders jumped 600 percent.

To activate the scarcity trigger, use exclusive information to persuade. For example, capture key decision makers' attention by saying something like, "I just got this information today. It won't be distributed until next week."

Be sure that the information is truly exclusive; otherwise, it could hinder your credibility.

Activating Audience
Self-Persuasion

I N MASTERING THE art and science of persuasion, you have a wide range of strategies at your disposal. These include establishing your credibility, understanding your audience, and capturing listeners' minds and hearts—as well as overcoming resistance and activating persuasion triggers. But there's another even more powerful technique: **audience self-persuasion**.

What is audience self-persuasion? It's a process in which you actively involve listeners in discovering the logic of your argument—in effect, getting them to persuade themselves. Persuaders use the following three techniques to transform listeners from passive recipients of a pitch to active participants in a dialogue:

- Visualization

- Questioning

- Active listening

Using visualization

Persuaders help audiences visualize the potential benefits of their proposals. For example, researchers posing as salespeople went door-to-door "selling" cable TV subscriptions. Some potential customers received a straight pitch stressing cable TV benefits. Others were invited to imagine how cable TV would provide them with broader entertainment. The results? Among people who received the straight pitch, only 19.5 percent signed up. Among those who imagined using the service, a whopping 47.4 percent decided to subscribe to cable TV.

Asking the right questions

Persuaders also use questions to engage audiences in a dialogue about their proposals. In fact, questioning counts among persuaders' most effective tools. Why? Many people enjoy answering questions. Having someone care about what they think makes them feel important. But the urge to answer questions also springs from the fear that others will look down on them if they avoid or can't answer a question. By asking questions, you control the content, pace, tone, and direction of the persuasion situation. You also determine which issues do—and don't—get discussed.

What kinds of questions best activate a listener's self-persuasion mechanism? There are several types you can employ:

- **Disturbing questions** get at the heart of your listeners' greatest concerns or problems. For example, suppose you're selling a parcel-tracking software system to a courier firm that's experiencing problems with lost and delayed parcels. You might ask your potential customer questions such as these:

  - "How much unproductive time does your staff spend locating lost parcels?"

  - "What effect is this problem having on your reputation with your clients?"

  - "Could this problem slow down your proposed expansion into new markets?"

These queries increase the magnitude of the lost-parcel problem in the customer's mind. They make the solution you're proposing more attractive and make the listener more willing to pay a premium to solve the problem.

- **Leading questions** influence how your listeners interpret facts and what they remember. They help plant specific information in your listeners' minds. For instance, suppose you're conducting a market study in which participants are viewing photos of a new product. You want them to notice and remember a particular feature of the product—for example, a special instant-replay button. If you ask, "How do you like the instant-replay button?" rather than "Do you see an instant-replay button?" your participants will be far more likely to remember the button after the study.

- **Rhetorical questions** enable you to give the answer after asking the question. These kinds of questions help push the listener into accepting a clearly defined proposition. Thus it's best to use them as you're summarizing your presentation or argument.

  Suppose you're seeking to persuade your subordinates to adopt a new way of processing orders. They've used the existing process for a long time, and some are skeptical about the proposed change. You present your case, and then you say something like, "We all know that order-processing errors have increased in the last two quarters. How else will we eliminate them if we don't overhaul the way we process orders?"

Listening actively

As your listeners respond to your questions, you, in turn, must become an active listener to further strengthen your presentation. Active listening means reflecting back and summarizing the content and emotions in your audience's responses to your questions. By reflecting, you show that you've heard and understood the other person—a powerful step in any persuasive effort.

Consider these guidelines:

- **Reflect content.** Paraphrase the factual details you're hearing from your audience, using language such as "It sounds like . . ." "In other words . . ." "So you're saying . . ." and "It seems that . . ."

- **Reflect emotions.** Acknowledge your listener's feelings. For instance, if an employee says, "I'm still doing the same old job. I could do it in my sleep," respond with, "Seems like you're feeling bored and frustrated. Is that it?"

- **Summarize.** To redirect a conversation that has wandered off track, sum up what you've heard so far. For example, "I'm concerned that we've gone off on a tangent. Let me see if I can touch on the main points we've covered." You can summarize at any point in a persuasion situation. But summarizing is particularly effective when emotion has begun clouding the issues or when you feel your views aren't being appreciated or understood. Summarizing is also helpful when you believe it's time to conclude an argument or when you've reached an agreement and want to ensure that you and the other party share the same understanding about the deal.

By using the techniques of audience self-persuasion, you further enhance the likelihood of moving listeners to your side.

Tips and Tools

Tools for Persuading People

Persuasion Self-Assessment

Use this worksheet to assess your persuasion abilities. For each statement below, indicate how accurately the statement describes you. "1" indicates "Not true"; "5" indicates "Very true." Be sure to answer based on your actual behavior in real workplace situations. In that way, you'll have the most accurate assessment of your skills.

Part I: Assessment

Statement	Not true		Rating		Very true
1. I appropriately establish my qualifications before I try to persuade.	1	2	3	4	5
2. When persuading, I offer proof of how people have been able to trust me in the past.	1	2	3	4	5
3. I analyze listeners' words and behavior to assess their decision-making styles and receptivity.	1	2	3	4	5
4. When persuading, I describe the benefits and unique aspects of my idea.	1	2	3	4	5
5. I use metaphors, analogies, and stories in my presentations to highlight my key points.	1	2	3	4	5
6. I limit the number of points I make in my presentations to no more than five.	1	2	3	4	5
7. I support my arguments with highly credible evidence.	1	2	3	4	5
8. When I cite facts, data, or statistics, I package the information for clarity and memorability.	1	2	3	4	5
9. I encourage feedback from my listeners to activate audience self-persuasion.	1	2	3	4	5
10. I use disturbing, leading, and rhetorical questions to encourage audience self-persuasion.	1	2	3	4	5
11. I actively listen to my audience and reflect the content and emotions behind their statements.	1	2	3	4	5
12. To determine my strategy, I analyze my audience before persuading.	1	2	3	4	5
13. I tailor my persuasion strategy, material, and approach for different audiences.	1	2	3	4	5
14. I vary my choice of media according to the message I want to communicate.	1	2	3	4	5
15. I help others in an effort to build trust and credibility, knowing that it could result in a relationship with others who will want to help me later.	1	2	3	4	5

Statement	Rating Not true → Very true				
16. I try to encourage people to make their commitments to my ideas publicly or on paper.	1	2	3	4	5
17. I tap the power that comes from titles or positions of authority that I hold.	1	2	3	4	5
18. When I possess exclusive information, I emphasize its scarcity value to those I'm persuading.	1	2	3	4	5
19. When I promote something, I stress that it's standard practice or part of a popular trend.	1	2	3	4	5
20. I associate myself with products, people, or companies that my audience admires.	1	2	3	4	5
21. I emphasize the similarities I share with people I want to persuade.	1	2	3	4	5
22. When I encounter resistance to my ideas, I use paraphrasing and questioning to understand the source of the resistance and to communicate my understanding of the resisters' concerns.	1	2	3	4	5
23. I try to establish positive relationships and feelings with people whom I want to persuade.	1	2	3	4	5
24. When I anticipate encountering resistance to my ideas, I raise and understand opponents' arguments before presenting my own views.	1	2	3	4	5
25. I use affirmative, assertive speech and win-win language while persuading.	1	2	3	4	5
Score for each column					
Total score *(Calculate your score by adding up the numbers in all your responses.)*					

Part II: Scoring

Use the following table to interpret your score.

104–125 **Exceptional:** You're a talented persuader with a solid understanding of the art and science of persuasion.

78–103 **Superior:** You're a highly effective persuader in many areas but would benefit from refining some of your skills.

51–77 **Adequate:** You know and practice many of the basics of persuasion. However, you can increase your success by further extending your skills.

25–50 **Deficient:** You'll need to work broadly on your persuasion skills to begin changing or reinforcing others' attitudes, beliefs, and behaviors.

Establishing Your Credibility

Use this worksheet to establish or enhance your credibility before exercising your persuasion skills.

Part I: Your Current Credibility Score

In the table below, list the names of the people you need to persuade to accept a proposition or idea. (Add more rows in the table if you need to persuade more people.) In the "Trust Score" column, rate how you think each person perceives your sincerity and trustworthiness. "1" indicates low; "10" indicates high. Do the same for the "Expertise Score" column. In the fourth column, calculate the total credibility score by adding together the "Trust" and "Expertise" scores.

Name	Trust Score (1 to 10)	Expertise Score (1 to 10)	Credibility Score Trust + Expertise Scores (1 to 20)
Example: Jane Sullivan	7	2	9

Part II: The Credibility Matrix

In the matrix below, place a dot for each person you listed in Part I, indicating how the person perceives your trust and expertise. For example, if you put a "7" in the "Trust Score" column for Jane, and a "2" in the "Expertise Score" column, you'd put Jane's dot in the lower right-hand quadrant of the matrix.

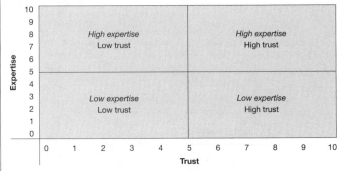

When you're finished placing a dot for each person in your list, notice where the dots seem to be clustering. Do you tend to have low perceived trust among your intended audience? Low perceived expertise? Low perceptions of both? Move on to Part III to see how you might strengthen any weak areas.

Part III: Credibility-Building Strategies

If you scored less than 11 for any of the names in the "Credibility Score" column in Part I, consider the following credibility-building strategies.

Tactics to Build Trust	Tactics to Build Expertise
• Be reliable. Do what you promise, and publicize your fulfilled commitments. • Be rational. Base decisions more on reason than emotion. • Be receptive. Show that you understand others' needs and concerns. • Always deliver more than you promised. • Have a trusted and respected colleague actively promote your reliability. • Acknowledge your failures and weaknesses.	• Publicize and distribute third-party testimonials that endorse your position. • Persuade a recognized outside expert to publicly validate and endorse your ideas. • Write and publish relevant articles. • Seek invitations to speak at important meetings and industry or professional forums. • Publicly celebrate early successes—even small ones—to prove your idea's value. • Learn to speak with flair, humor, and assertiveness on everyday issues. • Hire a coach or attend a course or industry conference to update yourself on cutting-edge thinking in your field.

In the planner below, list any problems you have with your perceived trust or expertise. Then list the actions you need to take to improve those areas.

Trust Issue(s)	Expertise Issue(s)

Actions Required	Actions Required

Understanding Your Audience

Use this worksheet to assess an audience that you will need to persuade.

Part I: Your Proposal and Its Benefits

What is the idea or proposition that you plan to communicate to your audience?

What do you hope to persuade your audience to do based on that idea or proposition?

List the benefits of your idea or proposition.

Part II: Audience Assessment

1. In the first column of the following table, list the names of the people whom you will need to persuade. These individuals include the following:

   • Decision makers—individuals who will approve or reject your idea

   • Stakeholders—people who will be affected by acceptance of your proposal

   • Influencers—people who have access to the stakeholders and decision makers and can sway their opinions

2. In the second column, list the benefits that you think each audience member values most.

3. In the third column, note how you would gauge each audience member's receptivity to your idea. Which individuals are hostile, supportive, uninterested, uninformed, or neutral?

4. In the fourth column, list each audience member's preferred decision-making style. For example, which individuals want a lot of factual information before making a decision? Which ones prefer to analyze other respected individuals' decisions and follow their lead? Which ones tend to feel enthusiastic about new ideas early on but then look for data to support the proposed idea? Which ones, in general, are initially skeptical of others' ideas?

Name	Benefits	Receptivity to Your Idea	Decision-Making Style
Decision Makers			
Stakeholders			
Influencers			

Part III: Action Planning

1. In the first column of the following table, copy the names of the individuals just as you listed them in Part II.

2. In the second column, note how you plan to win each audience member's mind. What benefits of your idea will you emphasize? What evidence will you provide to reassure your audience that those benefits are within their reach? What words will you use?

3. In the third column, note how you plan to win each audience member's heart. What vivid descriptions, metaphors, analogies, and stories might you provide to connect with your listeners on an emotional level?

4. In the fourth column, note how you plan to acknowledge resisters' concerns and communicate your understanding of their concerns.

Name	Actions to Win Minds	Actions to Win Hearts	Actions to Deal with Resistance
Decision Makers			
Stakeholders			
Influencers			

Part IV: Activating Triggers and Audience Self-Persuasion

What persuasion triggers might you set in motion before your presentation? For example, if you think the reciprocity trigger might increase your persuasiveness, what favors or kindnesses might you do for your audience members that would boost the likelihood that they'll support your idea in return?

How might you activate audience self-persuasion during your presentation? For instance, what disturbing, leading, and rhetorical questions might you pose to encourage listeners to persuade themselves of the value of your idea?

Test Yourself

This section offers ten multiple-choice questions to help you identify your baseline knowledge of persuading people. Answers to the questions are given at the end of the test.

1. What is persuasion?

   a. A process by which you change or reinforce other people's attitudes, opinions, or behavior.

   b. A process by which you quickly close short-term deals that benefit your company.

   c. A process by which you enable others to understand and support your organization's interests.

2. What are the two sources of credibility?

   a. Openness and candor.

   b. Confidence and assertiveness.

   c. Trust and expertise.

3. In any persuasion situation, your audience will likely consist of decision makers, key stakeholders, and influencers. Who are key stakeholders?

   a. People who have the power to approve or reject the change you're proposing.

   b. People who stand to be most affected by the change you're proposing.

   c. People who provide advice and information to key decision makers.

4. To win your audience's mind, you need to communicate the benefits of your proposition. Which of the following is an example of communicating benefits?

   a. "This new process is based on the leading-edge thinking in the field."

   b. "This new process uses a state-of-the-art database and the latest software."

   c. "This new process enables you to save time and acquire more customers."

5. One way to win your audience's heart is to change its organizing metaphor. Which of the following is an example of an organizing metaphor?

   a. "Management requires many different skills."

   b. "Management is a minefield."

   c. "Management gets easier as you gain experience."

6. In a persuasion situation, what should you do first to overcome resistance to your proposal?

   a. Understand the interests and emotions behind the resistance.

   b. Provide more evidence and examples to support your case.

   c. Candidly express your frustration to demonstrate your openness.

7. Psychologists have identified seven persuasion triggers—mental shortcuts your audience might take to decide quickly whether to support your proposal. Which of the following is an example of how to activate the liking trigger?

   a. You do small favors or suggest solutions for your intended audience that you believe will meet their interests and needs as well as serve your own interests.

   b. You make a connection between yourself, your company, or your product to individuals and organizations that the members of your intended audience admire.

   c. You discover common interests with your intended audience; express compliments; and make positive statements about your audience's ideas, abilities, and qualities.

8. Audience self-persuasion is among the most powerful persuasion techniques available. Which of the following is an example of something you might say to your audience that represents this technique?

  a. "Everyone knows that loyal customers generate the most profit. We've got to focus on customer acquisition."

  b. "What effect will losing ten clients have on your annual revenue generation?"

  c. "Would you like me to explain how this new process will solve your problem with customer defections?"

9. Which of the following is an example of how to establish your trustworthiness in the minds of your intended audience?

  a. Demonstrate your conviction and your openness to others' perspectives.

  b. Find out everything you can about the idea you're proposing—for example, by reading related articles.

  c. Retain the services of an industry consultant or recognized outside expert to advocate your position.

10. If you've determined that most or all of your audience will be opposed to the idea you plan to propose, how might you best structure your presentation?

  a. Help listeners visualize the bright future in store if they adopt your proposal, and tell them the actions you want them to take.

b. Describe a pressing problem that your audience is experiencing, and then present a compelling solution to the problem.

c. Present your opponents' position, and then refute their case by challenging their evidence and disproving their arguments.

Answers to test questions

1, a. Successful persuasion—changing others' attitudes, opinions, or behavior—can take place in a single meeting or through a series of meetings or discussions. Persuasion is about making a rational case as well as connecting emotionally with your audience. It's also about positioning an idea, approach, or solution in a way that appeals to or has value for the people who will be affected by it.

2, c. When you earn your audience's *trust*, your listeners consider your ideas and proposals. They see you as believable, well informed, and sincere, and they know that you have their best interests at heart. They also view you as possessing a strong emotional character (steady temperament) and integrity (honesty and reliability). When you establish your *expertise*, people see that you've exercised sound judgment, that you're knowledgeable about your ideas, and that you've accumulated a history of successes. Together, trust and expertise enable you to build credibility— an important foundation for any persuasion effort.

3, b. Although stakeholders—as the people who stand to be most affected by the proposed change—may not have the power to reject your idea, they can put up roadblocks to successful implementation of your idea if you haven't taken into account their interests and concerns. For example, if you're suggesting a new way of processing orders that will mean changes in the way your subordinates work, you'll want them to willingly adopt the new process after your decision makers approve its implementation.

4, c. Although an idea's features (such as how a new process works or what knowledge it's based on) may interest your audience, its benefits (how the idea will *help* them) most strongly attract listeners' attention. Persuaders who fail to answer their audience's question, "What's in it for me?" stand little chance of success.

5, b. An organizing metaphor is an overarching worldview that shapes a person's everyday actions and decisions. People reveal their organizing metaphors through the phrases and word pictures they use while speaking about the issue at hand. For example, a person who sees management as a minefield might say things like, "You never know when things are going to explode" or "You have to step gingerly when managing large projects."

To change someone's organizing metaphor, you identify a compelling replacement metaphor (for example, "Management is a playing field"). You then highlight the weaknesses of your audience's current metaphor and provide examples of people who have achieved success using your replacement metaphor.

6, a. By understanding the interests and emotions behind resistance, you can adapt your responses to win over your opponent. Paraphrasing is one way to uncover the source of resistance. You mirror what you think you're hearing from a resister (for example, "It sounds like you're worried about my proposal's impact on the budget"). If the person agrees that you've heard him correctly, you've created a small bond on which to build further agreement. The person will now be more open to considering new information or responses that you provide to address his concerns.

7, c. Liking is a powerful persuasion trigger. People tend to accept the ideas of individuals they like. Liking, in turn, arises when people feel liked by another person and when they share something in common with her. To activate this trigger, you create bonds by discovering common interests, and you demonstrate *your* liking of others through genuine compliments and expressions of appreciation.

8, b. This is a disturbing question—one of three types of questions you can use to activate audience self-persuasion. Disturbing questions magnify your listeners' problems in their minds, motivating them to persuade themselves of the value of your proposed solution.

In addition to using disturbing questions to activate audience self-persuasion, you can use leading questions to shape what your listeners remember ("How do you like the easy filing feature in this software?"). You can also use rhetorical questions, which give the answer you want your listeners to arrive at ("You've seen the mess our files are in; how else will we get organized if we don't start using this software?").

9, a. Demonstrating your conviction (your belief in what you're proposing) and your openness to others' perspectives is a good way to establish your trustworthiness in the minds of your intended audience. Additional ways to earn trust include following through on promises and commitments, sharing or giving credit to those who contribute good ideas, putting others' best interests before your own, and candidly admitting your weaknesses or faults. When you *behave* in a trustworthy manner, you earn a reputation for *being* trustworthy.

Combined with establishing your expertise, earning others' trust helps you build your personal credibility.

10, c. By presenting your opponents' position first, you show that you accept the validity of their position, thereby increasing their receptivity to you. As resisters become more receptive, they find it easier to hear you challenge their evidence and offer new and better solutions. When possible, be sure to incorporate resisters' ideas and suggestions into your proposed solutions.

To Learn More

Articles

Robert B. Cialdini. "Harnessing the Science of Persuasion." *Harvard Business Review* OnPoint Enhanced Edition (October 2001).

Cialdini shines the spotlight on persuasion triggers—the subconscious mental shortcuts people take to make decisions when they're pressed for time, fatigued, or distracted. Drawing from the behavioral sciences, Cialdini explores the following triggers: liking (people like those who like them), reciprocity (people repay favors in kind), social proof (people follow the lead of others like themselves), consistency (people align with clear commitments), authority (people defer to experts), and scarcity (people want more of what they can have less of).

Robert B. Cialdini. "The Language of Persuasion." *Harvard Management Update* (September 2004).

Suppose you are preparing for a potentially contentious meeting with someone you've worked closely with for years. It could be a fellow manager you want to convince to support an initiative but whose position in the matter is different from yours. Or it could be a long-term employee you're hoping will accept a new set of responsibilities that will take him away from his familiar, comfortable duties. Suppose, further, that you expect more than a little resistance. Is there anything you can say at the start of your meeting to reduce your coworker's reluctance to cooperate with you and your plan? There may well be a simple comment you could make that would incline your colleague to move willingly in your direction. To discover what to say, we need to leave the workplace and examine another context in which conflicting interests must be carefully negotiated: the romantic relationship. Learn to persuade others to your point of view.

Lauren Keller Johnson. "Tactics for Changing Minds." *Harvard Management Update* (June 2004).

As Howard Gardner, author of *Changing Minds,* explains, we find it increasingly difficult to open ourselves to new ideas as we age. Our worldviews ossify, preventing us from imagining something radically different. Resistance stiffens further if we experience unpleasantness after embracing an idea. For these reasons, leaders aiming to win support for their ideas can't rely on a single method of persuasion; they must draw on a well-planned blend of tactics tailored to influence disparate groups of tough-minded people.

Gary A. Williams and Robert B. Miller. "Change the Way You Persuade." *Harvard Business Review* OnPoint Enhanced Edition (May 2002).

The authors urge persuaders to tailor their efforts to their audience members' decision-making styles. Different individuals, they maintain, have different preferences for deciding whether to accept an idea. Each wants certain kinds of information at specific steps in the decision-making process. There are five styles that most persuaders will likely encounter in the workplace: (1) *charismatic* (easily enthralled but bases final decisions on balanced information), (2) *thinker* (needs extensive detail), (3) *skeptic* (challenges every data point), (4) *follower* (relies on his own or others' past decisions), and (5) *controller* (implements only her own ideas). For each style, the authors lay out corresponding strategies and examples of how to implement them.

Books

Howard Gardner. *Changing Minds: The Art and Science of Changing Our Own Mind and Other People's Minds.* Harvard Business School Press, 2004.

It is exceedingly hard to change people's minds. Ask any advertiser who has tried to convince consumers to switch brands, any CEO who has tried to change a company's culture, or any individual who has tried to heal a rift with a friend. Many aspects of life are oriented toward changing minds, and yet this phenomenon is among the least understood of familiar human experiences. In this book, eminent Harvard psychologist Howard Gardner, whose work has revolutionized our beliefs about intelligence, creativity, and leadership, offers an original framework for understanding exactly what happens during the course of changing a mind—and how to influence that process. Drawing on decades of cognitive research and compelling case studies—from famous business and political leaders to renowned intellectuals and artists to ordinary individuals—Gardner identifies seven powerful factors that impel or thwart significant shifts from one way of thinking to a dramatically new one.

Harry Mills. *Artful Persuasion: How to Command Attention, Change Minds, and Influence People.* New York: AMACOM, 2000.

Mills makes clear that anyone can learn to be a skilled persuader. In this book, he explores the psychology of persuasion and reveals how the most successful persuaders apply their skills. Exploring both the conscious and the unconscious forces at play, Mills provides practical guidelines for tackling the toughest challenges of persuasion, such as winning over hostile audiences, connecting emotionally with audiences, and getting your audiences to persuade themselves to support your ideas.

E-Learning Programs

Case in Point. Boston: Harvard Business School Publishing, 2004.

Case in Point is a flexible set of online cases designed to help prepare middle- and senior-level managers for a variety of leadership challenges. These short, reality-based scenarios provide sophisticated content to create a focused view into the realities of the life of a leader. Topics include aligning strategy, removing implementation barriers, overseeing change, anticipating risk, making ethical decisions, building a business case, cultivating customer loyalty, understanding emotional intelligence, developing a global perspective, fostering innovation, defining problems, selecting solutions, managing difficult interactions, applying the coach's role, delegating for growth, managing creativity, influencing others, managing performance, providing feedback, and retaining talent.

Influencing and Motivating Others. Boston: Harvard Business School Publishing, 2001.

Through the interactive fictitious case offered in this program, you discover how to motivate employees to excel, why leading employees is different from influencing peers, and how to persuade through negotiation and compromise. Numerous steps, tips, and tools help you start putting your learning into action. Based on the work of Jay A. Conger, Frederick Herzberg, Robert H. Schaffer, Roger Fisher, and Alan Sharp, *Influencing and Motivating Others* provides you with the concepts and techniques you need to hone your persuasion skills.

Productive Business Dialogue. Boston: Harvard Business School Publishing, 2002.

This program shows managers how to craft fact-based conversations, minimize defensiveness, and draw out the best thinking from everyone involved. *Productive Business Dialogue* introduces the *ladder of inference,* a tool that helps participants in a dialogue understand the distinctions among fact, interpretation, and conclusions; the program explains how clarifying these distinctions can dramatically enhance the productivity of meetings and discussions. Through interactive, real-world scenarios, you will practice shaping interactions that maximize learning and lead to better-informed decisions.

Sources for Persuading People

We would like to acknowledge the sources we used in developing this topic.

Robert B. Cialdini. "Harnessing the Science of Persuasion." *Harvard Business Review* OnPoint Enhanced Edition (October 2001).

Jay A. Conger. "The Necessary Art of Persuasion." *Harvard Business Review* OnPoint Enhanced Edition (February 2001).

"Handling Q&A: The Five Kinds of Listening." *Harvard Management Communication Letter* (February 1999).

Betty A. Marton. "Mastering the Art of Persuasion." *Harvard Management Communication Letter* (July 2000).

Harry Mills. *Artful Persuasion: How to Command Attention, Change Minds, and Influence People*. New York: AMACOM, 2000.

Liz Simpson. "Get Around Resistance and Win Over the Other Side." *Harvard Management Communication Letter* (April 2003).

Gary A. Williams and Robert B. Miller. "Change the Way You Persuade." *Harvard Business Review* OnPoint Enhanced Edition (May 2002).

Notes

Notes

Notes

Notes

Notes

Notes

Notes

Notes

Notes

How to Order

Harvard Business Press publications are available worldwide from your local bookseller or online retailer.

You can also call:
1-800-668-6780

Our product consultants are available to help you 8:00 a.m.–6:00 p.m., Monday–Friday, Eastern Time. Outside the U.S. and Canada, call: 617-783-7450.

Please call about special discounts for quantities greater than ten.

You can order online at:
www.HBSPress.org